#KNOWYOURROLE

"Every Woman's Little Black Book"

B. W. Blocker

ISBN-13   9780615433288
ISBN-10   0615433286

www.knowpink.com

#dedication

This book is dedicated to:

God, the one who which I adore, worship and appreciate, thank you for giving me purpose and life…

To my husband Odell, I love you and am honored to have been on this journey of life with you. You have helped me to learn and discover my "true" self. I thank God for your gift of compassion. You have opened my eyes to plenty and I look forward to many more adventures with you.

My two handsome boys, Caleb and Kobe, you bring mommy a little piece of heaven on earth with your presence.

My mother, Jacquelyn a woman of strength, you have molded me into the woman I am today. You pushed me to want more out of life and follow my heart. You birthed much more than a little girl that August. I appreciate your strength, courage, character and integrity.

My Father Ralph, one of the wisest men I have ever met. You were right; the past has to happen in order for destiny to take its place. Thank you for being there.

My sister, Candy, I thank you for your encouragement, support and calling me "Susie Homemaker." You rock and have been the greatest supporter a sister can ask for!

My best friends, Dawn, Katherine, Windy and Nicole; my goodness, all the memories that we have created and all the things that we have been through together, you ladies have always had my back. There is not a girl in the world that has the friends that I do.

To Ekaette, my spiritual little sister, thanks for your support, encouragement and deadline reminders! (LOL)

My cousin Leina Duncan, thank you for supporting me and sharing your poetry, the gift that God has given you with the rest of the world.

My Aunt Tonice for the helping with a perfect subtitle.

My Spiritual Parents: Rev. William A. Gray, III and Rev. Candace Gray you both mean so much to me. You have been my parents away from home. Thank you for your support and encouragement.

&

Pastor Trena Stephenson, thank you. You saw gifts in me that I did not see in myself. Thank you for your support, encouragement and allowing me to always be me. Thank you for keeping me in line.

#acknowledgements

To My Husband: throughout our journey together, I have learned so much about me. You showed me that true happiness really comes from within. You have helped me to realize that life is about helping others regardless of…
I love you and am so in love with you. I look forward to the rest of life's journey with you.

To Corey Smith: You have always been a big brother to me. Thank you for our many meaningful conversations about life, relationships and God. Well, due to that conversation in April 2010, at the moment, we both joked about me writing a book about women knowing their roles. Well…I Guess God is having the last laugh. Through our talk, this book was birth. Thank you for always being a good listener!

#KNOWYOURROLE
"Every Woman's Little Black Book"

By:
B.W. Blocker

Because I am a woman, I must make unusual efforts to succeed. If
I fail, no one will say, "She doesn't have what it takes."
They will say, "Women don't have what it takes."
Clare Boothe Luce

#tableofcontents

#foreword

In today's society, the role of the women is very vital to the functioning of our world. Mankind itself came through the womb of a woman. Many times however, the role of the woman is overlooked and not appreciated. We as women are mothers, entrepreneurs, ministers, wives etc. Our role requires us to be many things to many people at the same time. Imagine that we are jugglers, juggling many balls and wanting not one ball to fall. If one falls, one may feel that they have failed at the task.

Our role is one that is in high demand and often times very draining, yet fulfilling. We find ourselves looking for our true identity, not through the eyes of someone else but through the eyes of God. In this book, B. W. Blocker opens up her life before you showing her frailties, disappointments, and self-discovery; while finding her identity as a mother, wife, and minister of the gospel. You will cry, laugh and ponder on the life lessons and uncover pearls of wisdom she shares.

This book puts a demand on your heart to be honest with yourself first, then God. So, as you began to read this book, I ask you to open your heart and spirit to receive what God is trying to reveal to you about YOU. If you pull back the curtains of "I've got it all together" and the hard exterior women tend to put portray, the authentic you will spring forth.

Through the life lessons explored by B. W. Blocker, I believe that you will learn to discover balanced and grow to another level spiritually. However, you must open your heart to receive the messages. If you apply the pearls of wisdom shared within the pages of this book, you will be blessed beyond measure.

Trena D. Stephenson-Hancock, Overseer
Woman of God Ministries, Inc.

#preface

There are so many issues with which women have to contend. As a woman, there are challenges in handling multiple responsibilities we seem to face. Just understanding how to be, has become even more difficult. Then, of course, we are still the primary caregivers for our children, and now for some, our parents.

Being a woman in 2010 has made womanhood even more of a task. Quite often, we are hated because of an innate desire to create, think and transform our surroundings. We are misunderstood, just for being, however, we are somehow still able to exist and sustain our families and our womanhood. All this while we are berated quietly as well as admired for those very same traits.

To take all of the aforementioned issues and still proclaim God's word. To live it, to teach it, to preach it, and to model it can all be a very daunting task. Nevertheless, we rise to the occasion. We mastered what we did not realize, that being the ability to balance it all.

B. W. Blocker has managed to show us how to do that. Trusting that God will keep you in what He has called you to do, Blocker shares how we can do it all spiritually. She knows firsthand how to do some major balancing in her own life. Blocker will reveal how women can be all that God has called them to be and remain balanced in doing so. The book you are holding in your hands will mark the beginning of your journey to peace and of course balance.

May God bless your reading, and ultimately, your transformation!
Rev. Candace D. Gray, Assistant Pastor
St. Stephens African Methodist Episcopal Church

#intro

Everyday, millions of women play many diverse intricate roles in their daily lives. Society may call it the action of "wearing many hats," but it is much deeper than the metaphor of simple attire.

As a woman, I found it difficult to adapt and effectively act in my appropriate role at any given moment. When I was supposed to be a nurturer to my children, I was acting as a drill sergeant. When I was supposed to be a wife, I was acting like a detective. When I was supposed to be a Christian, I was acting as an egotist. The moment I realized that life was bigger than my current emotions, I was capable of performing effective self-evaluations. I no longer prayed that God would change others and fixed their flaws, I started to change the way I prayed, asking God to reveal, my own idiosyncrasies and imperfections. Once I started to realize that I was responsible for much miscommunication and self-caused irritations in relationships, was when my approach to all relationships changed.

When I started working on myself is when I started to accept responsibility and stopped being a blamer for unsuccessful relationships (not just intimate). When the dynamics of every relationship in my life started to change, I began to realize that all the chaotic moments in those relationships were moments when I was unable to define my role as a woman. So with prayer, God brought me back to the basics to help me to get to know me more, understand myself and allowed my life experiences to help other women to move toward bettering their lives, finding life's balance, grow in spirituality and improve relationships.

What does it mean to be a woman? Is it defined by sexuality or sexual characteristics, spirituality, feminism, womanhood, style, personality, nature, or it is the many roles we play every day? What are those roles and why is it important to understand them? The realization in comprehending the multiple roles that we play as women will help women better understand themselves, change life's perspective and improves interactions within relationships. So often women assumes their roles which allows them to function in areas where there is no need.

The purpose for writing this book is to help women discover the meaning of their role within relationships and how to effectively live and function within each appropriate role. Knowing your role is very essential and imperative to balancing out the overbearing woes of life. This is the key to improving any relationship, including the one you are developing and/or growing with God.

Reading this book is the beginning of an illuminating process of self-discovery, which will help you optimistically perform self-evaluations, embrace change, grow spiritually, and find a healthy life balance. Get ready for your journey!

#IAMWOMAN

By: Leina Raynell Duncan

Categorized and characterized

without having materialized
into existence
I am woman
With society's representations
I have been defined
and refined
Into the perfect feminine personification
But my self-perception
is only deception
For those unknown to me
You see
To carry the identification
"Woman"
Fits me with the description
That if I should refuse
I get no recognition
Woman, wife, mother, nurturer
Branded with labels
I'm expected to maintain
Along with the weight of the world
Keeping my emotions contained
I am woman
Never faltering
Forbidden from altering
The path already walked before me
For society has chosen
And this feminine pattern woven
To dictate my destiny
But now
I break free

I am woman
With the struggles of the world
I continue to survive
No longer looking for acceptance
Or tolerance
In your eyes
Disregarding the words you chose to
Identify
Me
No longer in your corner
Just settling for being content
I have come into my own
I have grown
I'm totally independent
My heart dictates my roles
My faith shall chose my goals
And I shall find acceptance
Within my own strength
Wife, mother, nurturer
That is me
Here I stand
I bare those labels
Because I can
A woman
Yes
I am

#KNOWYOURROLE

"Every Woman's Little Black Book"

#thewoman

"People are like stained-glass windows.
They sparkle and shine when the sun is out,
but when the darkness sets in, their true beauty is revealed only if
there is a light from within."

Elizabeth Kübler-Ross

What does it mean to be a woman? Is it emotion or estrogen? Is it anatomy or psyche? Is it defying expectations or responsibility? Is it beauty or boldness? Is it strength, sexuality, style, swag, or even stained glass windows, like the poetic words of Elizabeth Kübler-Ross. Defining what it means to be a woman has as many definitions. It would be much like trying to perform a head count of every woman to determine the total amount of women who roam the corners of the earth.

Nevertheless, it seems as if women have subconsciously sought the answer to the question when experiencing life's toughest moments and decision-making is the most challenging. Yet, shouldn't this question be equally as important, even when life is great. Why does it seem that the answer to this question is most relevant when life becomes chaotic or when a woman's role is being challenged? Experiences like physical, mental or verbal abuse, marriage, motherhood, friendships etc are all roles that are hard to juggle and find balance in that can cause a little stress on ones' life.

During life's challenging moments, issues of role reversal and other emotional roller coaster moments can cause the roles of women to appear unclear and undefined. It's time to discover who you really are and all the possible determinates that will prevent you from positive growth and role clarification.

The role of a woman requires multitasking and multi-role playing which is a tough task. Women are child bearers, emotional bearers, burden bearers and bearers of many things that people can't even imagine. Yet, what I have discovered is while going through difficult moments, knowing your role can be smothered by a title wave of emotions. The greatest question is: what is the role of a woman? Well, before we explore that, we have to understand the spiritual aspect prior to reading the definition.

In the second chapter in Genesis, after God planted a garden in Eden, he created man and placed him in the garden with instructions not only to work it but take care of it. When Eve was created, she was created as a companion and helpmate for Adam. Adam's role was to work and provide while Eve's role was to comfort and help. Each of their roles were very distinct. The true problem, now, is that women have operated in the man's role by working and providing. Some women have lost focus on doing what God created them to do. This doesn't mean you can't provide for your family or you must stop working, however sometimes life smothers the essence of the role of a woman which is to be a companion and help mate.

According to the Merriam-Webster dictionary, a woman is defined as an adult female person; belonging to a particular category; distinctively feminine nature; a servant or personal attendant.[1] Although this definition has some truth, in reality, being a woman is not defined by nature or ability to serve, but by her character, attitude, life, actions, style, appearance, home life and the company she keeps.

Many women may argue that some of these categories may not be relevant in defining the role of a woman. However, the

---

[1] "woman." Merriam-Webster Online Dictionary. 2010. Merriam-Webster Online. 1 October 2010 < http://www.merriam-webster.com/dictionary/woman>

truth is woman act in roles that reflect whatever life category they live in. Now is the time to step outside the box for a second to have a bird's eye view of ourselves. It's time for self-evaluation in which self-assessments can be positive or negative. On one end of the spectrum, some women can be too hard on themselves and the others, not capable enough to take responsibility for their actions.

Simply being a woman is like maneuvering a large umbrella that shelters an infinite amount of subcategories. Which of the following subcategories would you place yourself in: wife, girlfriend, homey and/or mistress, classy, sophisticated, complicated, educated, fashionable, cheap, vulgar, disorganized, manipulative, unpleasant, malicious, compassionate, spiteful, sensitive or supportive? There are thousands of subcategories in which women take refuge. These subcategories dictate behaviors, which define our roles in which we function.

Can two walk together unless they are in agreement?[2] Only you can answer that and how you answer, the question is based on individual perception. Regardless of whatever you may think defines a woman; it boils down to one simple answer. A woman is defined by her heart. Whatever a woman honors in her heart is the essence of who she really is. Most of the time, that essence is buried under traumatic experiences, pain, bitterness, broken hearts, disappointment, mistrust, skepticism, abuse and any other emotion that causes her to become a prison guard of her heart. It's time for you to unloose that woman because she has been held captive for far too long.

Whatever lies within your heart, that's what determines which roles you play, how you operate, manage, and function within those roles. Through my life experiences, I have learned that being a woman is not based on one attribute but multiple attributes either positive or negative. Those attributes are subconsciously ascribed a role. Those roles are determined by

---

[2] Amos 3:3 New King James Version (NKJV) Bible

experiences and have predictable behavior patterns that are usually determined by an individual's performance and social status.

The greatest advice that was given to me by two men, whom I don't think even they understand how much they have impacted my life. One of which is my pastor who taught me to always remember my purpose and the other is my former Clinical Pastoral Education Supervisor who taught me to always be aware of my role.

Knowing both, your purpose, and role in life are the major foundations of the reconstruction project of the real you. If defining a woman and her role were a simple task, then many relationships and lives would operate differently. There would be less tension, more patience and communicating with others wouldn't be so emotionally and physically draining. I asked some women what it meant to them to be a woman and here is what they had to say:

"What it means to be a woman, to be strong, independent, dependable, caring, forgiving, patient, kind and able to kick butt at the same time. My intelligence, my sincerity, my inner and outer beauty, my strength and my faith is what defines you me as a woman"

"It means being able to bring pure life into the universe. The ability to teach love, compassion and trust; It's the ability to reproduce makes for the continuation of humankind. And, by doing so, it is security for changes and in a more advanced phase. What defines me? I have never compromise myself for anyone or anything. Whether good or bad, I will never settle. I will not allow anyone or anything to leave me with such heartache or anger as to weaken me. I have learned that, as a woman, it is much better to release ill will, thereby allowing me to grow. As I have aged, I am more understanding and have learned to be patient. I give respect and expect it in return. And, the most importantly fact of all is that, I recognize that if not for God, none of this would be possible."

Finding the key to having peace of mind, true happiness and serenity is all done by unlocking the prison bars of your heart to free yourself and to begin to heal your emotional wounds. In true nature, many men view and deal with women in the same manner. Women are not created from cookie cutters, there much more like fingerprints. They look the same but in microscopic view are all completely different. We are all created with a uniqueness that every human being should respect.

We all can contest that being a woman is sometimes over bearing. However, being a better woman should be the goal for every woman. We all should strive for wholeness, spiritual stability and healing. The secret to finding a successful and meaningful balance in life is discovering more about your true self, learning how to heal your own wounds, developing a stronger relationship with God and knowing your role. It's time to unveil the reality that women play more than the role of a woman.

This book is a life tool to help women be better women, to have and choose healthier relationships and to discover life's balance.

#thepretender

"What the Heck is a Proverbs 31 Woman?"
Chapter 2

"For as long as you can remember, you have been a pleaser, depending on others to give you an identity. You need not look at that only in a negative way. You wanted to give your heart to others, and you did so quickly and easily. But now you are being asked to let go of all these self-made props and trust that God is enough for you. You must stop being a pleaser and reclaim your identity as a free self."

-Henri Nouwen

Maya Angelou describes a phenomenal woman in her infamous poem and the bible describes a virtuous woman in Proverbs 31, but what's the meaning behind all of it? In the beginning of my Christian journey, I assumed the definition and role of a virtuous woman, but truthfully, I did not want to know what it meant. In the beginning of my relationship with my husband, I didn't understanding my role as a woman. This sparked many arguments and also prevented me in taking responsibility for my own part. Not knowing my role as a woman and wife, resulted in a lot of miscommunication. Furthermore, at that point, in my life I did not care what a virtuous woman was nor about becoming one. I just thought that Proverbs 31 was another scripture trying to convince me to be more submissive to my husband.

The more we didn't get along, the more I rebelled at the thought of being anything like a virtuous woman. This rebellion caused me to become a pretender and it wasn't until I started proof reading this chapter that I realized it. When I went to church, family gatherings or anything else, I either didn't mention anything concerning my relationship or I pretended that it was the bomb. I guess it was more like a bomb hit it and blew everything up. During this period things seemed to be in pieces, appearing to be destroyed beyond recognition.

Being a pretender can cause one to personalize an experience and believe that they're the only person having or have had that experience. Many women pretend because of embarrassment, shame, guilt or for prestige. If the truth were told, we have all been a pretender at some point in our lives. It can be as simple as pretending we have a certain kind of prestige causing one to live beyond their means, or even pretending to understand what the heck a Proverbs 31 woman is.

Just in case you don't know, a Proverbs 31 woman is described as a virtuous woman of good character, strength, confidence, fearlessness, and faithfulness. She is a woman of moral excellence and righteousness. Being a virtuous woman is living in truth. In the beginning of my relationship and even early stages of my marriage, I pretended to know who I was and I had no clue. The only way I was able to function socially was to create another me.

Realize that pretenders create alter egos or characters that make public appearances to make others think that life is peachy and under control, even when others can smell the stench of chaos. You cannot find not an ounce of balance in this pretend role. Understand that pretending is detrimental to any friendship, relationship, and/or marriage. So many women are acting as if they want to continue certain relationships with fictitious loyalty, counterfeit trust, spurious needs, and mocked happiness. If you masquerade your personality and feelings about a person as well as the relationship, you are a pretender. If you really want to be freed from the claws of being a pretender, this is the moment when you would want to start being honest with yourself.

Countless times I have had women express to me that their perfect man suddenly changed overnight. Well, that may be how it seems but I can guarantee you, people don't change their personalities and behavior over night. That goes for you too! It seems as if the beginning is only a fantasy. In the initiating stages of a relationship, you work hard to make a good first impression for your partner, but it's also a chance to make a new impression for yourself. Pretending to have life all together without any, emotional baggage doesn't do you any justice. Most people pretend to protect the images that are trying to convey. The first impressions that resonate with others are the honest ones. For example, women hate men who pretend to have money and are broke; pretend to have their own place and live with their mom; pretend they have no financial problems and have bad credit. It's unfortunate that pretending hinders you from growing, allowing you to fall back into old habits and behaviors.

A comedian once said that when two people meet, they meet each other's representative. The representative is the pretender, wanting to show off all the good qualities while camouflaging the flaws of personalities, emotional wounds and idiosyncrasies until a later date. Should everyone have to RSVP to find out who you really are?

The role of a pretender creates a distorted reality that causes one to become a blamer and not one who takes responsibility and effort to change. The more I blamed, the less I was able to see my faults. I was unable to accept the reality of my relationship. Let me give you an example. A woman in denial, who has been told by an ex-companion that the relationship has ended, pretends and eventually convinces herself that she is still a part of an intimate relationship with that person. When this man is seen with another woman, it's viewed as cheating. The lack of responsibility is that the pretending woman never took the liability of providing self-care so that she could detach herself from the relationship and move on. Pretending is more harming than any other role in relationships. Not only can it can harm the pretender emotionally, it can harm the partner's relationship experience.

Being a pretender can cause one to build emotional barriers resulting in becoming a prisoner of self-blindness to the freedom that lies within reality. Anyone can ignore change, pretend to be happy, content or even make-believe that they are living a virtuous life. However, no human being ever reaches the level of perfection. We all change and need change. The goal is to always keep our spiritual eyes open and be ready to perform a self-evaluation to determine if we are operating in the role of a pretender or a virtuous woman.

A pretender's distorted reality may not always be spoken but communicated through actions. Behaviors like stalking, smothering, not respecting the other persons request for space or even "reverse psychology" are perfect examples. Pretenders often display arrogance and stupidity in their behavior. The pretender displays arrogance by thinking that the problems and issues experienced in the relationship are the fault of the other person. They display stupidity by choosing to be naïve and take the blame for all the problems and issues in the relationship.

Ask yourself this question: when you wake up in the morning, do you meet a representative in the mirror? It takes a lot of growth, maturity and courage to admit to being a pretender. Once you admit to being a pretender, you can do either one or two things: change or pretend that change doesn't need to take place. No one can have a true earthly experience if they live outside of reality. True reality is "virtuo-reality". It is being able to live in the truth of who you really are. It's acknowledging all your flaws, insecurities and idiosyncrasies, and at the same time, willing to do what is necessary to move forward, change and to annihilate old relationship killing characteristics.

What pretenders need to realize is that it's very difficult to have any confidence or find emotional stability in a relationship with a pretender. There is no long-term value in a relationship with a pretender because they can only manage short term relationships. The partner spends most of their time deciphering whether or not the relationship is authentic. Not only does being a pretender prevent spiritual growth, it causes one not to see the true value in relationships because of the constant functioning outside of reality.

Pretenders are not eager to change themselves. It's the reason why they are pretending, hence, the reason why complacency and spiritual laziness settles in. It takes less effort and energy not to change rather than actually doing something and become proactive about transforming one's self and the situation.

Operating as a pretender will often usher you into doing things you never thought you would do. It causes women become the opposite of what a virtuous women is. It's called adult peer pressure. Keep in mind that relationships are suppose to be rewarding not a task. It's hard work for a pretender not only because it takes tons of energy to continue a facade, but it's hard to attempt change due to compliancy. You may be growing in a direction of leaving the club life or a promiscuous lifestyle (not just sexually) and because the company you keep makes you feel uncomfortable about your attempt to create new beginnings, you settle.

I challenge you to not only step into your role as a virtuous woman but to read Proverbs 31:10-31 everyday for 31 days to witness a positive approach to life and personal relationships change. When you keep the truth in the forefront of your mind, you function in it. Then you can determine whether or not if you want to be a part of the relationship. Stop pretending, start practicing and develop the habit of accepting reality. Here is a list of steps you can take to take charge of your journey:

∂ Perform routine self-evaluations to see if you can discover your own areas of improvement.

∂ Ask for the input of others and create a list of collective issues in areas of improvement. Without being defensive, analyze the issues and make a great effort into trying to avoid having them again.

∂ Develop techniques on how you can effortlessly create successful relationships.

∂ Start taking responsibility for what you do and for what you want.

∂ Lists the things that make you happy and do more of it.

#thewife/girlfriend

"Do more than belong: participate. Do more than care: help. Do more than believe: practice. Do more than be fair: be kind. Do more than forgive: forget. Do more than dream: work."
William Arthur Ward

Maybe the famous author William A. Ward was on to something with making this statement. Being a woman in a relationship is being more than a giver or taker, its being a participant and helper; one who practices kindness, forgiveness with forgetfulness and goal orientated. With all that being said, it's easier "said than done" to incorporate all of those into a relationship? Better than that, how can women put forth this type of effort in a relationship without feeling it in return?

Have ever heard of the 50/50 rule? It's the rule created for ideal relationships! It is a guideline for communication in which provides a balanced scales of fairness and equality within a relationship. The 50/50 Rule rules out biases, assumption, rudeness and even impulsive behaviors. During many memorable moments in my life and discovering the real meaning of the 50/50 rule, I realized that I had many misconceptions about what the rule meant. Here is what I thought about the 50/50 Rule:

∂ Both partners equally share household responsibilities.

∂ Both partners equally share duties when children are involved.

∂ Both parties equally participate in decision making: not making decisions without the other

∂ Being equally yoked in religious beliefs.

∂ Equal amount of effort to making the relationship work: Being on the same page.

∂ Equaling sharing financial responsibilities.

Surprisingly when it came to financial income, I wanted to opt out of my half or adopted the "what's yours is mine, and what's mine is mine" concept. It's amazing how the 50/50 Rule is completely ignored when it applies to income. Anyhow, you may be thinking or agreeing with some of those thoughts and may have tried to incorporate a few of them within your relationship.

Let me clarify the real definition of "The 50/50 Rule": The 50/50 Rule consists of the following: 50% of you putting all efforts into the relationship and 50% of your partner doing the same thing. It's the essence and blueprint of balance in a relationship. Both partners have to be 100% willing to make the relationship, contributing 100% of their efforts work in order for the rule to help your relationship grow to a level of success.

How can you apply the 50/50 Rule to a relationship that you already involved in? Even though marriage or long term relationships is about unity and union between two individuals, remember all relationships have boundaries. The key to applying the rule is being willing to put your own pride despite the negative display of your partner. Most of time when there are misunderstandings and arguments within relationships, the 50/50 Rule is violated because of two things that happen: role reversal and boundary crossing.

When there is a rule violation, you have to not react in a negative way, but allow yourself to process the situation and deal with it with the rule's definition in mind. If not, it may appear that you are challenging the role of your partner. Challenging the role of your partner during conflict is like adding fuel on a bonfire. Things like telling the "man of the household" that he is not because of financial contributions. Keeping the 50/50 Rule in mind at all times will prevent you from becoming narrow minded to the possibilities of change and prevent you from harboring a negative spirit that causes your partner to not want to be in your presence. When healthy boundaries are established, you will be able to create and maintain a healthy intimate, physical, emotional relationship with your relationship partners. Identify if you have healthy intimate relationship at this time. Healthy boundaries let you choose who you allow into your space and how they treat you and help you figure out who you are as an individual and what treatment you'll accept from other people.

Along with developing health boundaries, the 50/50 Rule is the "knight in shining armor" for all relationships. This rule is the single most difficult rule for many women to apply to their relationships. Before we unveil how to apply the 50/50 Rule to your relationship(s), here are elements the rule requires.

∂   Humility
∂   Patience
∂   Being an "Emotional Listener"
∂   Respect
∂   Spiritual Obedience
∂   Patience
∂   Love/Compassion
∂   Empathy
∂   Patience

Without a thought, many women assume that incorporating those elements causes one to go back into the role of a woman from the 1950's. Don't be afraid of the word submission. In saying that, remember that you should never be a "doormat" for anyone! Ask yourself: what is your fear of submission? Is it pride or fear of feeling emotionally vulnerable? Or, is the person you are submitting to worthy enough of your submission?

Gender roles and relationship responsibilities have always been a topic of discussion for ages. I can only imagine King David and Bathsheba discussing what responsibilities they would split or Oprah and Stedman's conversation regarding the head of the household concept. Understanding the differences between men and women is accepting the differences in thought process, sensitivity, memory, and communication. A successful relationship it's pertinent that both partners recognize and discover the meaning of their roles, differences and the true meaning of the 50/50 Rule.

In the beginning of my marriage, "The 50/50 Rule" was one issue I squawked about the most. Tackling issues such as sensitivity, communication and even styles of problem solving was often addressed in my marriage, however not as much as the 50/50 Rule. Over time, after many discussions, arguments and disagreements my husband said something to me that was so profound. He said, "When I have to shovel the snow or patch a roof are you willing to help me with doing 50% of the work?" My immediate response was, "heck no!" Sounding like Mr. Miyagi speaking to Daniel-san, he followed up by saying, "exactly, my 50% is providing and operating in the areas that you are limited or aren't willing to do and vice versa." After trying to convince me to opt to trade responsibilities, I declined. I realized that making sure the kids were warm and cozy while drinking their warm milk wasn't an even trade for shoveling snow. Just because the jobs are different and have completely different mental and physical effects on the body, both are equally important to positively keep the household in function.

The 50/50 Rule never limits possibility neither places glass ceilings over spousal roles. Depending on the dynamics of your relationship, both partners need to have a level of understanding of each other's role and responsibility within the relationship. Take the time to think about not only your partners' efforts but yours as well in making the relationship work. If you feel that there is not effort, then address that rather than attacking other issues that are not important. Address the real issues that you have, not in a nagging way but with a solution or ideas on how both, you and your partner can improve the relationship. There should be no tyrant ruler within a relationship or household, however there should be a responsible leader.

I have to honor my belief and say that I believe that a (responsible, sensible, respectful, well-rounded) man should be the leader of a married household. In honoring that, I know that my role as a woman in that house makes it a home! It's the woman who makes the home run effectively and efficiently.

Don't get caught up in the "wife/girlfriend" title and think that you have won the game. Titles come with responsibility. For example, a doctor has a title, but it's how good he/she is at the job that receives flourishing amount of patients. Just the title alone is not enough. If I said I was a doctor, you would ask what type? Well the same applies to wives and girlfriends. How good are you at your job?

Every relationship requires work and every job requires a form for skills to be improved. Here are some helpful tips[3] that you should implement into your role as a wife/girlfriend:

∂ Do not take an argument into the bedroom. Both of you need to make this rule firm and clear. Your partnership needs a place to be nurtured a place that is sacred and protected from all the day-to-day troubles of life. Make that place your bedroom. If in fact if you are busy like most of people are and you are having trouble keeping up with the housework, make sure that your bedroom is always free of clutter, the bed is made and the room is

---

[3] Nessi. "Beyond Jane." 10 Tips to Being a Good Wife. November 29, 2007. Accessed 15 January 2011 <http://beyondjane.com/family/marriage/10-tips-to-being-a-good-wife>.

generally clean. Make this a place you both love to escape to at the end of the day to spend time together.

∂ Never put your husband down in front of people. You would not like it done to you so do not do it to him. This is the man you love, treat him accordingly.

∂ Remember why your husband is working. It is not to spite you. It is improve the standard of living for both of you. Do not add to his burden by making him feel guilty for being at work. If you feel he is overloaded, and perhaps the stress of it all is getting to him, talk to him about taking a weekend off; ask him to schedule sometime in the near future. It may be a month away but at least you will both have something to look forward to.

∂ Plan activities in your free time together that you will both enjoy, or at least make sure that the time is equally divided into things you enjoy and things your husband enjoys doing. Do not over schedule the free time you have together with visiting relatives and other social obligations. Try to nurture your relationship.

∂ When your husband has time to spend at home do not overload him with so many chores that he is looking forward to Monday morning when he can return to work and take things easy. Talk about what things need to be done, offer to set up a schedule, find out what he wants to do and plan the jobs accordingly. You may even find its better to hire outside help. This is something you need to discuss.

∂ Maybe not flowers, but remember men like surprises too. Perhaps tickets to a sporting event, rent his favorite movie, a special lunch time surprise at work, even a simple text message to tell him you love him and you a looking forward to seeing him later.

∂ His friends may be horrible, but they mean something to him. Do not put them down, or make fun of them. Would you like him to treat your friends that way? If he does, perhaps you need to discuss that you do not like it and agree for both of you to stop.

∂ Finally, don't nag it causes wrinkles!! (Joke) However, I promise your mate can do without it!

Love him in spite of all of the flaws and create a life of love around your relationship.

#thedetacher

"From Coal to Diamond"
Chapter 4

"Our life is full of brokenness - broken relationships, broken promises, broken expectations. How can we live with that brokenness without becoming bitter and resentful except by returning again and again to God's faithful presence in our lives."
-Henri Nouwen

Waking up at 3:41a.m., I did what most people do and checked my Facebook page. I was catching up, reading and commenting on friends' status updates and I remembered that my brother-in-law had an interesting post. He responded to a questioned that someone sent to his inbox while playing the infamous game of Q and A. Q and A is a game of questions and answers when a person sends you a message asking you questions of any sorts. After you get the question in the inbox, you post the question and answer as your updated status without revealing the name of the person who asked the question. It's very amusing, if I may add! Anyway, while playing this friendly game of Q and A, he posed this status:

Q: "What do you want in a relationship?" In a timely response, he gave a list of "normal" things and characteristics that are his preferences for dating a particular type of woman. His answers are as follows:

"1) Trust
2) Someone that understands my needs and wants...someone who desires what I am willing to give
3) Someone who has a relationship with GOD
4) Someone who is patient
5) Kind

6) Someone who has a good relationship with their dad/or dad figure
7) Someone with an upbeat bubbly personality
8) Someone with vision...and a nice smile"

Immediately, a woman asked about the relevance of #6. I must admit, I was going to ask but wanted to see if someone else would first. He responded by stating,

"...a father or strong and consistent male presence in a girl's life does have an effect on her self-esteem and I also think that a female can learn a lot about how to interact/communicate with a strong male from witnessing their mom as she compromises and negotiates with dad as they work through issues."

Who knew that at 3:41a.m., that I could receive a divine revelation from a facebook status? When I read his status, I felt like I had a personal realization. Maybe my brother-in-law was onto something. As I pondered and immediately did a self-evaluation, I realized that the tone of many of my relationships had a direct connection to my own relationship with my father. I remember at one point in my life, as a young adult, when I would encounter difficult moments in relationships, or if there were some trust violation, I would immediately emotionally disconnect. I had learned to successfully detach myself from the any relationship that could potentially cause me to feel any hurt. As I got older, I dealt and managed relationships according to a "severed leg" policy. Once there was a relationship violation, I would sever the relationship and the person completely from my life, which prevented emotional connections, relationship healing, and the process of forgiveness to take its course.

My relationship with my dad is and always has been great, however when I would get mad, or disappointed in a decision that he had made, I would be quiet through the conversation, walk away and if it was really bad, not call for a week or two. I developed serious bad relationship habits even before I was in any serious relationships. As an adolescent, I learned that when I was emotionally rubbed the wrong way, the next step was to detach myself to prevent feeling any emotions about the situation or the person. I did this not as a punishment, but because I was ignorant. It's amazing how God reveals our blemishes to us decades later.

At the moment I wrote this chapter, I realized how God had to "un-teach" me about my own bad detaching relationship habits and how I use to act solely on my emotions. Reacting emotionally had become a bad emotional attachment becoming the main source of impatience. I began the process of thinking about things, relationships, and potential opportunities that I may have walked away from prematurely as a result of my emotions. The revelation in all this is that a detacher's passion and past can cause current disturbances in any relationship, marriage or friendship.

No matter the circumstance, every relationship needs to have these tools:

∂ Communication
∂ Witnessing Positive Interactions
∂ Compromise and Negotiation

When these things are absent is when one is apt to willingly and /or selfishly choose to become a detacher. I know personally so many women that are currently playing the role of a detacher in marriages/relationships, who truly love their partners but are completely disconnected emotionally and/or physically. It's common to see a partner in marriages/relationships that emotionally split when infidelity or even trust issues are acknowledged. As a result, one of the ways of coping with the relationship violation, the partner emotionally detaches. The real question is: why?

Over time, women have learned to detach themselves from a persons or relationship as a defense mechanism to protect her from feeling neglected, unappreciated, unheard and unimportant and from any other emotional traumatic experiences. The unfortunate realism about this being a detacher's role is that it's hard to turn off and on. The emotions of a woman who is a detacher causes her emotions to spill into many aspects of her life and relationships

From personal experiences, the only way I was able to free myself from being a careless detacher, was learning how to forgive. Along with deepening my relationship with God, the concept and process of forgiveness helped me to understand me, better. What I've learned is that forgiveness is one of the most compassionate things that we can do for ourselves. The truth about forgiveness is that it requires a level of compassion, and the reason why people become detachers is because of the lack of compassion that was shown toward them. We tend to think of forgiveness as an act of kindness that we choose to give to some people who seem to deserve it, yet withhold the gift from others who seem un-deserving and un-repentant. This gives us a significant sense of power and control! Forgiveness actually has nothing whatsoever to do with other people and has everything to do with the person giving forgiveness.

In the book of Malachi 3:17 NKJV states, *"They shall be Mine," says the LORD of hosts, "On the day that I make them My jewels. And I will spare them…"* We are God jewels, and if we as women want to move from having an unforgiving heart of "coal" to be the diamonds (transparency and all) that we were created to be, we must starting forgiving and start moving towards going through a spiritual mining process.

So many women in relationships are just diamonds in the rough: unpolished, unshaped, unrefined, untreated, untouched, and unreformed. They are un-buffed rocks that neither they nor their partner has had a chance to discover the priceless beauty that lies beneath. Diamonds are found within the depths of the earth. They are found close to the surface through deep-origin volcanic eruptions. The magma for such a volcano must originate at a depth where diamonds can be formed.[4]

Just like diamonds, God sees us before we are cleaned, buffed and polished. If He sees the value in us, why is it difficult for us to see true value in "worthy" relationships that we should reattach ourselves? In the early stages in my marriage, I viewed my relationship as having no value. It wasn't until I prayed, changed my relationship approach, and practiced forgiveness; I was able to see the relationship's value and the priceless value of my husband. (Ok vultures, don't even try it!) It was in that moment that I moved from "coal" to diamond status. Trust me, it wasn't easy. Understand that there are certain steps and processes that all diamonds go through before you see the beauty shown in store cases. Diamonds aren't as beautiful when found, but they are cleaned, buffed, and polished. Refined diamonds attract millions today.

In order to move from coal to diamond status, it requires you to understand who you are. Geologists argue that diamonds are known for being the strongest, hardest, unalterable and unbreakable natural substance on the face of the earth. This sounds similar to the hearts of so many women in "functioning" relationships. I would contest that the hardened heart of a woman could probably crush a diamond. I have heard throughout my life from many men and women that "hell has no fury like a woman scorned." Nevertheless, no one addresses healing the heart of that scorned detached woman.

There is true healing in forgiveness but it is a personal decision to make. Trust me, the true words from a former detacher, forgiving others will help you gain a part of your "true" self in return. Freedom lies within forgiveness because you will no longer

---

[4] Erlich, Edward and Hausel W. Dan. *Diamond Deposits: Origin, Exploration, and History of Discovery.* Littleton: Society for Mining, Metallurgy, and Exploration, 2002.

view the world from a victimized perspective while being freed from the claws of angry.

The moment I started to exercise the power of forgiveness and faith, believing that God will protect me was the moment I started to trust myself with trusting people more. I gave God all the power and responsibility for severing toxic relationships that were unhealthy for me. This allowed the process of unhealthy relationships to end naturally without leaving the taste of the bitterness in my mouth. It's important to realize that protecting yourself in the manner of detachment is a control issue. It's a way of depowering the other person (friend, father, mother, sister, cousin etc) or issues in your life and a way to strengthen your internal self. Women have discovered this new way of being able to partake in relationships without the investment of vulnerability.

So here is the fork in the road in this book. If you are not interested in repairing your emotionally detached personality and relationship traits in your relationships, then I suggest you skip to the role of chapter 6: the walker. However, if you are interested in repairing your relationship read on.

I recently read and discovered some valuable pieces of wisdom that I call "pink-golden" nuggets. in an internet relationship forum by an anonymous writer. The writer states that "culturally, self-reflection and exploration are seen as indulgent or wasteful, yet we are pressed to enter into emotionally committed relationships before we've given ourselves a chance to explore who we are, what we believe and feel at our cores, what our strengths and frailties may be. Often relationship struggles are the outer reflection of our inner struggle to find and define self. Secondly, relationships are hard because they require balancing two basic and conflicting human drives: the need to be a separate, autonomous self (and the individual freedom this implies) with the need to be connected with others (and the compromise/negotiation it requires)."[5]

Henri Nouwen, an internationally renowned priest, author, professor and pastor said "Our life is full of brokenness - broken relationships, broken promises, and broken expectations."[6] How can we live with that brokenness without becoming bitter and resentful except by returning again and again to God's faithful presence in our lives? To affirm Nouwen, there is no way one can live an emotionally stable and healthy life with brokenness. It's like trying to live life with an untreated, uncovered bullet wound. With a constant pain, you eventually become numb and ultimately bleed to death. You can use all the boxes of band-aids your little hearts desires, however, without the proper hospital treatment and a good surgeon, life isn't promising. Using that in context, emotional wounds are like bullet wounds. Life threatening and eventually you become numb from the pain. They require the proper treatment, care and God being the emotional surgeon, life becomes promising.

Always keep in mind that each relationship has different dynamics but the role you play within each is always consistent. Revisit your past to see if it has any input on the roles you play as an adult. It's important to remember that in order for your relationship to grow and mature you must nurture, treat, and allow God to heal your emotional wounds so that you will no longer be a detacher.

---

[5] Anonymous. "Are Relationships Supposed to Be Easy?" Online posting. n.d. Relationship Quotes. 23 Nov. 2010. <http://www.latestngreatest.net/relationship_quotes.htm >.

[6] Nouwen, Henri. "Belief Net." Quote Library. n.d. 12 Dec. 2010 <www.beliefnet.com/Quotes/Christian/H/Henri-Nouwen/Our-Life-Is-Full-Of-Brokenness-Broken-Relationsh.aspx>.

Here are tips on how to begin your emotional healing and to find balance in your life and relationship:

∂ Research and inquire about personal, relationship and/or Pastoral Counseling to help you during your healing process. Being a detacher is learned behavior from your past.

∂ Deliberately try to change your focus: every time you start to focus on the relationship or the person, intentionally redirect your thoughts and energy on something else.

∂ Learn to trust yourself more: Depending on the health of your relationship, allow yourself to be a little vulnerable in promising relationships.

#theinvestor

"Deposits and Withdrawals in Relationships"
Chapter 5

"Understanding how to be a good investor makes you a better business manager and vice versa."

Charlie Munger

According to Webster Merriam Dictionary, an investor is one who commits (money) in order to earn a financial return; to make use for future benefits; advantages or to involve or engage especially emotionally.[7] Using this term in context while making it relevant, a woman who plays the role of an investor is one who commits (to any activity), tries to make use of her qualities in hopes that there would be an interest for future benefits, and becomes completely engaged and emotionally involved. While looking for love, the investor invests herself completely, willing to take the risk of rejection or even failure in a relationship. Instead of allowing a crappy business deal to flow like water under the bridge, the investor invests more in hopes of a return or success.

What investors need to be aware of is the power that lies within this role. This role is one that operates out of risk, expecting a profit and if one is not careful, this role can dominate your personality and cause one to become a user and abuser. The dynamics of this role demands the balance of virtuous living. Too many women are investing what's sacred (time, intimacy and love) into relationships that aren't promising and have little to no growth potential.

---

[7] "investor." Merriam-Webster Online Dictionary. 2010. Merriam-Webster Online. 1 October 2010
<http://www.merriam-webster.com/dictionary/investor>.

One of my best friends always used this saying when giving advice: "why would a man buy the cow if he can get free milk." This is so true. Ask yourself, to whom and how are you investing yourself? Are you investing yourself in something/someone that has growth probability? It's very important to be able to recognize and determine what you will gain (unselfishly) out of every experience. Not only is life about change and constant growth, it's about investing yourself fully so that you get the best out of it.

Investment manager and philanthropist, Charlie Munger's business philosophy was that incentives explain why people behave the way they do. In context, women need to allow "incentives" to manifest with in relationships before they fully invest. What will you gain (long-term relationship, partner, security, stability, trust etc.)? How you invest and how you view what you are investing in determines how successful it will be. It's ok to invest commitment, care, compassion or sex but realize that those things should be done after careful evaluations are done to see of the investments are worth it.

A numerous amount of relationships crash and burn moving one into an emotional recession, which is caused by the mismanagement of the relationship and the misunderstanding of self-worth. If you ever sit and think, what successful business investor or company continues to invest in a non-profitable project? If a hamburger place was unsuccessful selling burgers, and only thieves showed up to steal profitable resources, the company would close due to lack of profits. Logically, the investors would revamp the plans, reevaluate the project to see if it's worth continuing, and then proceed to make a decision. A true investor recognizes a win, a loss and is willing to correct the loss by reconstructing a new plan.

There should be no difference between the rules for business investors and the rules for relationship investors. The rule and definition of an investor should be consistent no matter the context. If a woman invests herself in any way in a friendship or relationship that is proven unsuccessful, why should she reinvest more of herself, in hopes of a profitable return? It seems as if revamping the plans, reevaluating the relationship and determining the potential are overthrown by denial. Often so many women are unwilling to accept the fate of a failing relationship no matter the emotional toll and how it affects their ability function on a daily basis. A true investor neither allows abuse of power nor allows leaching thieves to steal her joy, destroy her esteem or break her beyond the point of possibly being healed.

Its time for investors take position and do some relationship evaluations. Relationships that you profit happiness, peace of mind, joy and pleasure is a keep, relationships that are draining, chaotic, stressful, demanding and abusive are discontinued. Are your current friendships and relationship worth your investment?

On the other hand, are you even worth someone else's investment? Is your attitude and/or behavior a reason why you don't have customers/relationships? Potential customers love strong, independent, self assured, consistent, loyal investors, not crazy ones! True investors just don't dive into a project. They evaluate it to determine its growth potential and worth. I can see how many men are turned off when they meet women who 100% invests her body, emotions and self on the first or second date. What you have to offer can be seen as a gain in a relationship. Deposit the real you into your relationship and allow your relationship to mature so that withdrawing a commitment is the result. Accrue your interest and allow your mate to withdrawal commitment out of it.

It's impossible to think that someone can get to know the real you overnight. As a matter of fact, it should be considered an art to be able to reveal the real you and at the same time not scare the other person off. To think that someone could potentially see value in you when you haven't discovered your own self worth is ludicrous.

Here are some tips on becoming a successful investor in a health relationship:

∂ First Impressions: Everyday is a new a "new" day. Be pleasant, kind and compassionate towards your mates needs. You know what they say, first impressions are lasting impressions. Be patient, pleasant and persistent in acting as if you already are receiving the future benefits. Everyday act from love.

∂ Communication: Instead of telling the other person to improve in their communication, work on your own.

∂ Investors need to be good listeners. Don't always assume what you think your mate wants from you. Observe, ask, listen and be willing to compromise.

Everyone wants to find the best way to invest their money to let them make large profits and become rich but very seldom are women aware of the types of their relationship investments and possible profits. There are many ways to invest and each individual investor has preferences and different views towards the risks involved. The stock market is the first thing people think of when they decide to invest. Aiming for higher standards and greater profits, the key is to buy low and sell high. Invest small and then gradually make greater investments over time, which requires patience. Do the same in your relationships, be a smart investor!

#thewalker

"The single most powerful tool for winning a negotiation is the ability to get up and walk away from the table without a deal"
- Anonymous

If you love someone, can you walk away from an unhealthy relationship? The answer to this question is based on who is answering and the condition of the circumstance. If answering for a friend, your answer may be based on logic. If answering for yourself, your answer may be based on emotion.

The "oh-so" popular role of a walker has been functioning in the wrong manner for years. It's a role that women play when they are willing to accept the reality that a particular relationship is unhealthy and willing to walk away.

The majority of women that I meet doing ministry all agree that walking away was either not an option or the most difficult thing that they could not stomach to do. Many based their answers on financial circumstances, children, or contentment. I always find it amazing how life often has a way of unveiling the reality of unfitting relationships. It seems as if some women have blinders over their eyes, believing that time will make an unhealthy relationship healthy. These women hope for platinum rings to validate engagements or crave matrimony ceremonies as is they were magic potions to heal and detoxify contaminated relationships. It seems that in today's society working through toxic relationships is the "normal" in thing to do. A classic diagnoses of the "stick it out" syndrome.

One of the greatest things I have learned about love and all of its unspoken rules it is that it's flexible. Walkers need to stop self-negotiating to find reasons to stay. You can very well love someone and walk away from an unhealthy relationship. You can love them enough to walk away because you want to see them happy even if it means that it's not with you. Love is about partnership in a relationship. In 1 Corinthians 13, the bible tells exactly what love is; therefore, we can conclude what love isn't. Love is not a prison or place to keep anyone in emotional or spiritual bondage. One of the most powerful things that I have discovered in my relationship with God is that God would never abuse, misuse, mistreat or disrespect me. He wants me to have an abundant life. So if God offers me happiness, why should I accept anything less in any relationship?

Knowing when it's appropriate to walk in the role of a walker can be very complex. Additionally, a woman who possess the intuition to walk away and leave unhealthy relationships is one of the greatest attributes that a she could possess. Unfortunately, many women don't exercise it.

Have you ever seen the movie the Negotiator with actor Samuel L. Jackson? In this 1998 film, Jackson was a skilled police negotiator that finds himself falsely accused of embezzling funds from a police pension fund. He's so thoroughly framed that he must take extreme measures to prove his innocence. Although he is accused of corruption and murder, he takes hostages in a government office to gain the time he needs to find the truth. The same way Jackson diligently tries to prove his innocence is the say way you should be diligent about your well peace of mind and well-being. Happiness is not up for negotiation.

Women have learned to adapted, tolerate, manage, and be manipulated by toxic relationships. Often women find themselves fighting daily on the battlefield of life, defending their womanhood, character and demanding to be respected. Threw my life experiences I have learned that all battles aren't meant to be fought. Being a walker takes having some moral fiber. If not, then you can risk becoming cold hearted and unforgiving. It should never affect your pride, esteem or self- worth. I have meet and counseled women who have wanted to call off their weddings and walk away from obviously unhealthy relationships. However, because they felt embarrassed and were concerned about what others would say, they went on with the wedding. What many women fail to realize is that walking away doesn't determine the destiny of the relationship. If it was meant to be, it will be. I never said that this role was an easy one. It's a role that requires constant prayer and faith in God to develop enough courage to take a risk much like an investor. Walking away is not a sign of weakness it's a sign of faith in God and strength. Knowing when to appropriately walk away temporarily during an argument or stride permanently away from any unhealthy friendship or relationship is the key.

In order to find balance for this role, unveiling the camouflaged shackles of emotions is a must. What is keeping women from walking away from toxic relationships?

∂   Hopefulness
∂   Denial
∂   Fear
∂   Doubt
∂   Love
∂   Finances

If you feel that any of these things are a basis for your decision to leave a toxic relationship, then your decision is not on logic but emotions. As human beings, if we all based everything on our emotions this world would be a wreck! For example, emotionally choosing not to go to work because of the unsettling effects of an argument or break up with a companion. That will only last a few days until you logically reason and rationally think. Then you start to think logically about your vacation or sick leave and financial effects the choice has on your life. Eventually you move from using your emotions to using your logic to make decisions. Eventually, you will be able to push through your emotions, go to work, function normally, and emotionally adapt to the situation.

The key to being a walker is finding the positivity and balance in this role. Understand that the role of the walker exercises flexibility. Just make sure the change is positive and healthy. Martin Luther King, Jr., once said, "Faith is taking the first step even when you can't see the whole staircase."[8] To find balance in this role, one must have to develop a strong-mind, will, courage, and sincerity in your approach to end all injurious relationships while trusting God to comfort, provide, and protect you.

Here are some helpful tips:

∂ Set high standards for yourself. You want to be with someone who treats you with respect and dignity. Don't want to settle for less than you are worth.

∂ Leave on good terms instead of waiting for the hatred to set in. Recognize when you aren't getting what you need from the relationship. Follow your gut instinct instead of waiting until the perfect time to end the relationship.

∂ Be realistic. Don't try to trick yourself into thinking that things will eventually work out. If it is meant to be, then the relationship will be. Remembers successful relationships are not forced.

∂ Walk away if someone else is involved in the relationship. Show a cheater that you expect to be respected and treated decently. You can give the person a second chance if they are truly sorry but don't stay if the cheating continues.

---

[8] "Good Reads." Martin Luther King Jr. > quotes . n.d. . 20 Feb. 2011
<http://www.goodreads.com/author/quotes/23924.Martin_Luther_King_Jr_ >.

∂ Plan to get counseling for yourself and for your children if any. Even if relationship counseling doesn't work, therapy can help you adjust and process the change.

∂ Think about the future in a positive way. Value your independence and embrace the changes. Look ahead and see yourself happy when someone new walks into your life.

∂ Get your priorities and finances in order. Get your financial concerns in order and make sure you have a place to live. Take care of your basic needs like food and shelter.

#theaccepter

"The Root of Codependency"
Chapter 7

"Co-dependency can be defined as the tendency to put others needs before your own. You accommodate to others to such a degree that you tend to discount or ignore your own feelings, desires and basic needs. Your self-esteem depends largely on how well you please, take care of and/or solve problems for someone else (or many others)."

Edmund J. Bourne

Every woman at some point in their life has played the role of an accepter. The accepter role is one that is often played by choice and had little to do with personality traits.

The accepter has two traits: 1) one who permits and accepts any inappropriate behavior from another, distorts their own reality to find an excuse to rationalize another's wrong behavior. 2) One who accepts mistreatment and permits inappropriate behavior from another because of low self-esteem or fear of losing the relationship. The question is at what point in our lives does playing this role get tired and old.

On this stage of life, the accepter is one who allows reverse psychology and misdirected blame to conjure up a false reality that never existed. For example, your friend catches your mate cheating and tells you about the cheating. You call your mate to tell them what your friend has seen. After telling you that it isn't true and your friend is lying, in the back of your mind you start second guessing the words of your friend causing to evaluate the trust and loyalty in your friendship. A classic case of "if you don't see it, it doesn't exist!"

Although this may be possible, however, you don't always have to see evidence to know that something exists. Wind exists and you never see it; all you see is just a product of its power. What I'm trying to say is trust your God given instinct. It's called the gift of discernment. Trust in what you see and feel and trust God enough that you can not only stand on your own two feet if you need to use them, but also trust in God enough to provide for all of your need and desires.

So many woman tolerate mistreatment, abuse (verbal and physical) and inappropriate behavior because they want to "feel" like they have somebody. Well, what good is having someone around you physically if there are with someone else mentally and emotionally? Being the acceptor only causes inaccuracy in really dealing with the reality of the circumstance. It clouds the ability to clearly think process and decide what is best for both partners. Every relationship is diverse and has different dynamics. What may work for you and your relationship will not work for someone else. No one decides to be an acceptor. It seems as if this role is one that sneaks up on us. It slowly morphs and becomes a part of the personality when dealing with certain individuals. When we are acting in this role, we usually are amped to do things we said we would never do. Acting outside of our selves, accepting behaviors and consequences that we said we would never accept. Nevertheless, we are left stunned and amazed wondering how we have gotten to that point.

When you are co-dependent, you are typically looking outside yourself for definition or a sense of self. It might be through material things or the roles you play in life. You might also look for a sense of identity through a relationship with another. This allows shame and embarrassment to settle in which ushers a woman into one or two ends of the spectrum: isolation or untamed behaviors. Turmoil in relationships is to be expected. Your response to the chaos determines the destiny of the relationship as well as how you manage other relationships in the future. What a woman is willing to accept from her mate is based on how she values the person and the relationship. The value of the relationship is determined by how vulnerable you are and how much of your true self and emotions you have exposed.

Don't approach or look at every person that you are attracted to as a potential mate. Let time expose the motive and then evaluate to see if there is potential. Get to learn and know the person and their personality, likes and dislikes. Give yourself some time. Women need to stop living life as if there is an hourglass full of sand that determines our life's timeline. Marriage, children, security, and stability are things that are exposed and discovered in a potential mate's characteristics over time. Under no conditions should we ever become accepters of stupidity but accepters of reality. All the things that you are looking for in potential make allow those things to manifest over time and stop trying to "man make" them in your time. Time reveals potential.

Some unspoken reasons why women choose to be the accepters is due to traumatic emotional experiences in their past. Usually toxic unhealthy relationships are fueled by disrespect, power struggles and attempt to control the person while claiming that love is the foundation while you feel emotionally out of control. Your goal should never be to suppress your emotions or happiness but to pursue it by any means necessary.

The balance for an accepter is to learn how to let go of toxic relationships, be comfortable with the decision, and don't renege on it. In toxic relationships, accepters are not skilled when it comes to limits, boundaries, or letting go. Accepters get addicted and have issues of neediness that cause them to avoid letting go of unhealthy relationships.

The technique in identifying if you are an "accepter" in a toxic relationship is by self-evaluation to determine if you feel like you are losing yourself to the control, wants, temper, and/or abuse of another or if you are the one becoming abusive.

Realistically, it's easier said than done when learning to let go. Trust yourself and learn how rebuke and release toxic relationships while accepting and embracing positive change. Don't wait until you hit rock bottom to start your change. The time is now!

Here are some tips and techniques to better embrace positive change in your life and relationships:

∂ Make a list of the things that you want or need to change to improve your life and set both short-term and long-term goals.

∂ Make great attempts in breaking bad habits, even in areas of your relationships (making excuses etc). Many studies show that habits are broken and formed in very similar ways. It has been said that it takes 21 continuous days to form and/or break a habit. Start now.

∂ Reward yourself for even the smallest victory. Find something you enjoy and treat yourself.

#theneedy

"Codependency"
Chapter 8

"For as long as you can remember, you have been a pleaser, depending on others to give you an identity. You need not look at that only in a negative way. You wanted to give your heart to others, and you did so quickly and easily. But now you are being asked to let go of all these self-made props and trust that God is enough for you. You must stop being a pleaser and reclaim your identity as a free self."

Henri Nouwen

In Nouwen's book, *The Inner Voice of Love: A Journey Through Anguish to Freedom*, he eloquently describes the philosophy of a co-dependency. The writer's quote seems to all point to the reality of the natural difficulties that manifest in co-dependent relationships. In my opinion, if there is ever a role that could handicap a woman it would be living in the role of the needy. The ever so popular role of the needy is one of the most popular roles played by women.

The reliance of two people on each other in a relationship should be equal. However, when one partner pulls more on the other in a needy way, it can initiate harmful behavior patterns. One thing that I have discovered when helping others sort through difficult relationships is that co-dependency is a learned behavior that can be passed down from one generation to another. Mental Health America describes co-dependency as emotional and behavioral condition that affects an individual's ability to have a healthy, mutually satisfying relationship.[9] It is also known as "relationship addiction" because people with codependency often form or maintain relationships that are one-sided, emotionally destructive and/or abusive. This behavior is learned by watching and imitating other family members who display this type of behavior.

The role of the needy and co dependent behavior usually becomes a parasite on one's personality sucking the life out of your true personality. If the needier ever were to dig to uncover the core of being needy, one would discover tons of emotional baggage. It probably would look like presents under a Christmas tree at a rich woman's house. Although wrapped in pretty packages, gifts of neglect, mistrust, insensitivity, spite, bitterness, and anger were delivered from the Santa Clauses of past relationships.

The root of emotional baggage causes one to be needy. Being needy makes one seek validation and reassurance from an individual in hopes to destroy the feeling of being alone or lonely. I can definitely say that I have lived with a house full of people and still felt alone. Being with a mate does not cure the wounds of being needy and feeling alone. The mate only becomes a band-aid on wounds that only you can heal.

I often witness women who function in the needy role often compromise themselves and their beliefs as well as voluntary choose to be in unstable relationships. I have heard women say things like: "I need a man to feel complete", "I need to feel loved", and the most infamous, "I don't want to be alone." Regardless of the circumstance, acting in the role of the needy makes one desire to be in any kind of relationship and/or continue unhealthy relationships. Being needy sends batman signals in the sky to heartless users and abusers.

---

[9] Unknown. "Mental Health America." Co-Dependency. n.d.. Mental Health America. 11 Nov. 2011 <http://www.mentalhealthamerica.net/go/codependency>.

Most women that I know and have met that are "needies" are often stuck in this role especially in new relationships. Neediness is a turn off to most people and can be very unappealing. The key is to depend on God how you depend on that other person. He will never get tired of your calls. To find a balance for this role or free you of it completely, here are some healthy tips.

∂   Find Your Spiritual Dependence!

∂   Deal with emotional issues with spiritual and/or therapeutic counseling to help deal with issues of rejection.

∂   Be Patient: Stop forcing things to happen. Allow them to happen naturally.

∂   Take Your Shades Off: Part of the reason we get disproportionately excited in new relationships is because we tend to "idealize" a person in the very beginning. Be patient and allow the natural process of acknowledging a connection (other than sexual) with them.

∂   Get Busy: Fill in the gap. Idle time can cause you to over call, text, visit, or tweet. Find something that you enjoy doing. Spend time with yourself. If you invest the same amount of time that you do getting to know someone else, you may get to know yourself more.

∂   Learn to trust: This does not mean be naïve! Once you start dealing with your own flaws, issues and emotional baggage then you can start to sort out issues you might have in relating to the other people. Neediness is often associated with a shortage of trust, and sometimes a fear of abandonment. When you find yourself doubting someone's feelings for you, or their loyalty, ask yourself why you don't trust them.   Is it because they did something questionable? Or is it because someone in your past hurt you?

#theother

*"The people we are in relationship with
are always a mirror, reflecting our own beliefs,
and simultaneously we are mirrors, reflecting their beliefs. So...
relationship is one of the most powerful tools for growth.... If we
look honestly at our relationships, we can see so much about how
we have created them."*

Shakti Gawain

*"Power is my mistress. I have worked too hard at her conquest to
allow anyone to take her away from me."*

Napoleon Bonaparte

Surprisingly, performing research, I discovered several interesting definitions for the word mistress. According to Merriam-Webster a mistress is 1) a woman who has power, authority, or ownership 2) a female teacher or tutor: a woman who has achieved mastery in some field 3) a woman other than his wife with whom a married man has a continuing sexual relationship. [10] I guess all of the definitions are fitting for the role of a mistress in addition, all of these definitions have strength in contextual framework: power, ownership, mastery and sexual relationship.

In my quest for the truth, I asked a series of questions to get the opinions of men and women regarding women who play the role of the "other" woman also known as the mistress. I asked the questions using facebook as my resource because it's the fastest way of getting accurate survey results in a timely manner. Take a

---

[10] "mistress." <u>Merriam-Webster Online Dictionary</u>. 2010. Merriam-Webster Online. 30 November 2010
<http://www.merriam-ebster.com/dictionary/mistress>

look at the questions and anonymous responses from the feedback. All responders were instructed to respond privately in my inbox so that answers wouldn't be shared. The following questions were asked:

What is a mistress? How do you feel about having or being mistress? Why?

"A mistress is someone who thinks they can take the place of being the wife in a marriage situation. Yes I was one and my thought at the time was I could do it better than the wife and do things that the wife would not do."

"A mistress is an adulterous and home wrecker and so is the man. If a man thinks he needs a mistress he should release his wife to avoid the hurt caused by these relationships. I would never be a mistress or second to no one. I was taught early that you never see a married man on Sunday's and Holidays and I believed it then and I believe it now. I am too good a woman to settle for foolishness."

"To me a mistress is a woman with no self worth and low self-esteem. She knows deep down, whether she is in denial or not, she is not number one. And as a woman, she should know how devastating and awful what she is doing is for the other woman and her family. It's really quite sad. Did have a boyfriend once having this emotional affair with another girl (no sex, just talks). Dropped him like a sack of potatoes the same day I found out. Next! LOL :)"

*"A person who is aware that he/she is in an involved with someone who is in a relationship. If my mate had a mistress I would be upset and heartbroken. I never been a mistress and don't inspire to be one. Well, come to think of it when I was messing with *****, I also felt like he was lying about still being with his baby's mother. I could never prove it, but I had to leave him alone because he was full of it. So in a why I guess I felt like I was a*

mistress and wasn't cool with it cause I knew I deserve more than just being second or the other women. "

"A mistress is the side woman who messes with someone's husband knowingly. I have never been a mistress...well, does that include even if you're not married? I never known my partner to have a mistress because they are what they are mistress they are kept a secret at all times, so who knows if he had one or not. The one time I did mess with someone knowing that he was in a relationship, it was such a headache. I will never do that again...ever...I think it is so wrong. But I think you can only be a mistress if you are married; and heck no, if I knew my husband had a mistress I would not continue on with him at all...why would a person want to continue a relationship knowing their man is with another woman...I know my worth and it's not being with someone that I know has a mistress.."

*"Well, I think that a mistress is a woman or man who knowingly engages in a relationship with a man or a woman who is already committed. I believe that it is very wrong to deceive the other person in the relationship. However there are some relationships that are open and that other party may not mind his or her significant other to be with someone else. I personally being a mistress was not enough; I'm very selfish and could not be in the background. I was very young and dumb and didn't realize what I was agreeing to. So put the shoe on the other foot and I'll probably ********* if I found out! That relationship lasted for about 3 months, I think revenge on my ex and I realized that I was worth more, I met my husband a little bit after that!"*

As my inbox flooded, more woman than men had much to comment regarding this issue. I probably could have done an entire book with just comments regarding the "other" woman. It seems as if wives/girlfriends are operating on defense rather than on offence charging to win the game. I must say surprisingly, that wives were more fearful while mistresses were calm, relaxed and confident. Confusing!

Nonetheless, when writing this chapter and addressing this role, I had the privilege of interviewing a woman who is currently a mistress to a married man for over 20 years. During the interview I realized that my initial attempt in writing this chapter was done from a wife's perspective. After that interview, and the interviews that I had with men who had affairs with married women I was able to take a much more neutral position on the topic. I opted to break this role up into three parts: The Other: Mistress, The Other Wife, and the Unknown Other.

"The Other: The Mistress"

Mistress: A woman with a power that attempts and participates in an inappropriate relationship (seductive phone calls, exciting secret dates, gifts and the thrill of doing something bad) with a married man while seeing him in secret to have a romantic and sexual relationship.

The "Other" Wife

"Other" Wife: As a result from being detachers within a marriage, the "other" wife is a married woman who becomes a mistress to other man (single or married). This woman has power but lacks self-control by attempting and participating in an inappropriate relationship with another man while seeing him in secret to have a romantic and sexual relationship.

Much like the mistress, married women usually don't seek to be another man's woman. It seems as if there is an emotional disconnect within the relationship with the husband, the woman adjust and adapt to the role and modified their lives to fit.

The "Unknown" Other

"Unknown" Other: A women who get involved into relationship not knowing that the guy is married or is in a "common law" relationship.

Each of these sub-roles has one thing in common: POWER! Millions of books about "why men cheat" or "how to prevent your man from cheating" have been sold from millions of bookshelves. It's time for women to move from the "why" to efficiency and self improvement. Focusing on changing and bettering you is the single most important thing that you could to improve your relationship.

Pink Golden Nuggets:

The power that is given to mistresses is actually given to them by the other women. In every conversation with married and single men, each of them has stated that they really didn't want to cheat or have a mistress. The primary reason why they ended up in having an outside relationship is due to a lack of something at home. I know many I may catch some flack about this statement but it's a part of reality. What men really want is to be with the one that love and have invested their time.

Here is what some men had to say about what they wanted from their relationships:

"Support and Encouragement; we like to feel appreciated. It seems that no matter what we do right women focus on what we did wrong."

"Just someone who can help me become a better person, someone I can grow together with can tell me when I am right or wrong..."

"Personality, drive, compatibility and humor"

"Simple things: A woman that men know they can count on. Who can feed them spiritual, emotional, and sexually. Being there when the going gets rough like in this economy. In reality what men want and it's just like the song says a lady in the street who can handle all adversities, able to give us insight when in need but at the same time able to allow us to be the man even though they might be the ones with all the answers…"

Men really aren't as shallow as women think. Every man that I interviewed said that when the woman that they loved lacked the ability to give those simple things, along with communication (the #1 answer), this marks a point in the relationship when is when the cheating begins. In one interview, one married man stated that "the mistress is dressed for success." There is so much truth in that. The mistress knows her role and plays it well.

Ladies, it's time to be YOUR husband's (fiancé etc) mistress. Think about it, the mistress is always presentable, well dressed and looks her best, non-nagger, compassionate, flexible, cooks, supportive, willing to buys into his dreams and goals, spontaneous etc. If you were your husband's mistress, how could the other woman have anytime to be the mistress!

Being your husband's mistress requires some dual role activity. Not only can it spruce up your sex life but also it can help balance out your permanent role as a wife. So often, our other roles can cause lose some of our true personality and spontaneity within the relationships. In all the areas that wives/girlfriends lack, the mistress is willing to make up. Now realistically, wives can't be 100% perfect. I do believe in the 80/20 rule, which in context means that persons in relationships put forth 80% of their "good" genuine selves in the relationship. The 20% gap is due to human imperfections that we just cannot control because people just are not perfect.

On the other hand, what I have discovered in helping couples revive their relationships is that many wives have admitted to putting in less than 50% because they were not happy with the behavior of their spouse. Well, unfortunately, one of you has to be the person who makes the "big" step toward maturity and give it a try.

From conducting several interviews with women who are mistresses I have realized that not any of them set out in life to be a mistress. The moment that wives/girlfriends stop worrying about WHY men cheat and start focusing on being the best woman he can be for her is when role clarification becomes clearer.

Use the role of the mistress to your advantage. Don't "hold out" on intimacy as a punishment because that's not what a mistress would do. Don't use the silent treatment and/or not preparing a meal as sources of punishment because that's not what a mistress would do. Don't be a reality dream killer when he dreams of starting a business, that's not what a mistress would do. The role of being the "other woman" can be played by you to your mate if you choose to. Dual roles = Power

More Pink Nuggets:
- ∂ Pay attention to the needs and modes of your mate. Know when to be the wife and/or nurturer and know when to be the mistress.

- ∂ Know when to voice your thoughts in a non-nagging way.
- ∂ Be emotionally available for your mate. Many times the world beats him down enough. Receiving a beat-down at home is not needed could be damaging.

- ∂ Know when to give his space.

- ∂ Know when to be supportive: you don't have to be the mind of reason and reality all the time. Help him dream.

- ∂ Cook: Not just the same old meals. Get new recipes and try new things. Every once in a while, put on a pair of pumps and make up on when you cook. Men love food, a beautiful woman and a full tummy. Monotony in food is a terrible combination with a monotonous relationship!

The moment that a woman has a self revelation of the power that she possesses is the moment she can redefine herself and the roles that she plays in an unquestionable manner. The power that lies with being a woman is just simply being the best woman. Although it appears that, the "other" gets the hassle free relationship but at the end of the day to whom does he go home to? If it's you, then you have a chance to win him over. Remember the mistress and pride is your competition and you determine if you put in humility and love enough to win him over. The combination of these roles is imperative to achieving and grooming successful relationship. Healthy power is blinding.

There are three zones when dealing with the balancing of power for the wife acting as her husband's mistress in the relationship:

∂ Intimidation: risking the lost of a great, healthy and balanced relationship is risky. A man who has a complete package (according to his standard) is least likely to risk losing the relationship.

∂ Positive Accusations: Without being naïve, don't be so quick to think that he is out doing negative things. Use positive reinforcement and positive thinking. Using positivity can cause him to keep you in mind when tempted to make risky decisions and judgments.

∂ Gratification: Look for the positive things in the current relationship. Increase your appetite for happiness, enjoy and pleasure rather than sucking the life out of life. The essence of power is using it in a good way to really achieve balance.

∂ Intimacy: Not just sexual. Men love women who listen and who is willing to develop great communication skills.

If you want to improve your relationship, a part of balancing out your life is to change your perspective of it. If you never change, then you will always get what you always have gotten.

#theabuser

"True Balance is in Self Care"
Chapter 10

"Woman is more fitted than man to make exploration and take bolder action in nonviolence... There is no occasion for women to consider themselves subordinate or inferior to men....
Woman is the companion of man, gifted with equal mental capacity....
If by strength is meant moral power, then woman is immeasurably man's superior....
If nonviolence is the law of our being, the future is with women..."

M. K. Gandhi

"Self-compassion helps to eliminate a lot of the anger, depression, and pain we experience when things go badly for us," says psychology professor Mark R. Leary of Duke University.[11] When you practice self-compassion and self-love, you:

∂ Feel less anger, frustration, and pain, depression.

∂ Blame yourself or beat yourself up far less often.

∂ Get defensive or irritated with people less often.

∂ Struggle less with painful memories (real or imagined).

∂ Accept responsibility when things go wrong.

∂ Deal with negative emotions in healthy ways.

Have a self-perspective that doesn't depend on the outcomes of events – but rather on your own positive view of yourself. Often times when we think of abusive situations, we think of male

---

[11]Leary, Mark R. "Self-Compassion May be More Important Than Self-Esteem in Dealing With Negative Events, New Studies Show. ." Duke University: Office of News and Communication. . 17 May. 2007. Duke University. 23 Feb. 2011 <http://www.dukenews.duke.edu/2007/05/selfcompassion.html>.

"violence" (mentally and physically) towards female or even vice versa. Never once have I thought about "self on self" abuse.

"Ms. Do Too Much"

In the process of writing this book, an academic thesis, an additional 10-page paper, managing my household, traveling, and working, and the list goes on, I realized that I was doing to much. During all of this, my body had the nerve to get some violating virus that made me really sick. The nerve!!! I realized that I was abusing myself mentally and physically. I had literally "ran myself into the ground" until I got to the point where I was sick in the bed and could not move. At that moment, I reflected on something a co-worker said to me. He said, "You better learn how to take care of yourself, or you will regret it when you are older. You better learn how to take better care of yourself!"

His words were words of simplicity but some of the wisest words that I have heard in a while. He was right! I realized that self-care is not only important for you but for your relationship! If you are worn out, no energy, exhausted, agitated, irritated, and whatever other emotion we could possibly experience at the time has the ability to suck the life out your true personality. We as women have to learn healthy ways to pour positivity, energy, and vibrancy back into ourselves through self-care.

In an internet article, author, Elizabeth Scott, expresses the importance of self-care. Many of us have so many responsibilities in life that we forget to take care of ourselves. While it's hard to prioritize something like taking a bath when you have so many other priorities in life, self-care is an important aspect of stress management. A massage, soak in the tub or other forms of pampering revitalize you inside and out. Taking time out to treat your body like the temple it is has other benefits:[12]

---

[12]Scott, Elizabeth. "Take Care of Yourself: You Deserve It!" Stress Management. 12 Jul. 2007. About.com. 1 Feb. 2011 <http://stress.about.com/od/lowstresslifestyle/a/selfcare.htm >.

∂ **Self-Care and Your Physical Health**: While self-pampering doesn't always lead to major improvements in overall health the way healthy diet and exercise do, the relaxation you get from it can trigger the relaxation response, which can prevent chronic stress from damaging your health, so in a sense, self-care is good for you inside and out.

∂ **Self-Care and Your Emotional Health:** Taking time out to care for yourself can remind you and others that you and your needs are important, too. Having a well-cared-for body can make you feel good about yourself and your life, and conveys to others that you value yourself. This can contribute to long-term feelings of wellbeing.

∂ **Self Care Makes You a Better Caretaker:** People who neglect their own needs and forget to nurture themselves are at danger of deeper levels of unhappiness, low self-esteem and feelings of resentment. This affects your relationships! Sometimes people who spend their time only taking care of others can be at risk for getting burned out on all the giving, which makes it more difficult to care for others or themselves. Taking time to care for yourself regularly can make you a better caretaker for others.

It's so important to take time out for you. Along with prayer and meditation, taking a time out is another effective way to manage stress. Taking care of yourself will help you to be an effective partner in your relationship.

"Ms. Procrastinator"

Being a procrastinator is just as abusive as having no time for self-care. Procrastination has a definite negative effect on our personal lives. It is very abusive to continue to put your body through this type of stress, not only is it unhealthy for you; it puts unnecessary strain on your relationships. The true question is, "why put things off to the last minute?" This puts unnecessary stress on your body that eventually causes you to become impatient, agitated and short tempered with others. It would be ideal to go to sleep while our personal assistants magically complete every task on our list, but in reality, most of us do not have personal assistants like celebrities!

I don't think we realize the amount of stress and/or anxiety we put on ourselves when we procrastinate. I remember I once had several assignments, papers and bill payments all due on the same day that I put off to the last minute. This became extremely stressful for me to manage. Everything that could have gone wrong that day did. As a result, my procrastination created a more stressful environment for myself and my family. The stress created from procrastination is something that does not motivate us to become more competitive or innovative, but something that can drive us into a mental institution.

I read an article once that said that the moment when we convince ourselves to procrastinate, we aren't doing anything but deceiving ourselves into thinking other things are more important than what we should be doing at that time. One reason we are so easily distracted is because of our lack of self- control. In order to get more out of life, we may want to learn how to better control ourselves, especially when it comes to our personal finances. If we are procrastinating when it comes to paying the bills, this can lead to mounting debt, which may have lasting effects on us. This debt not only affects us it may affect our children and loved ones.
For example, if you accumulate some bad debts, it's possible that your children may inherent your debt and therefore are responsible for it. That's not a burden you want to put on your kids just because you were being irresponsible. Or if the mortgage is not paid in a timely manner, the bank or mortgage company may proceed with a home foreclosure.

So as you can see, it is very easy to tell ourselves that we will pay that bill later or put the check in the mail tomorrow. What's not easy though is dealing with the consequence of getting the check in the mail too late and losing a home as a result.

Procrastination is the road block to life balance and a stress free life. The only tool you need for this role is a lack of laziness. Here are some techniques:

∂ Cut out distractions.

∂ Cope with anxiety. One of the major reasons for procrastination is the fear that the job won't be done well, or it may reveal a new set of problems. Prepare yourself for these problems, rather than avoid them.

∂ Get rid of any ideas that lead to perfectionism. There's no such thing as perfection. Complete the project the best you know how, but realize there will be flaws.

∂ Set realistic goals. Don't expect too much out of a project and you won't be disappointed. Take the project one step at a time

∂ Ask someone to hold you accountable. While doing do, don't procrastinate asking for help!

Take better care of yourself. It makes you a better partner, co-worker, friend, mother, sister and caregiver.

#thehealer

"The Wounded Healer"
Chapter 11

"A woman is the full circle.
Within her is the power to create, nurture and transform."
Diane Mariechild

I received a phone call one evening from a woman whom I admired. In our conversation, she shared some things about her childhood that were very traumatic. As a little girl she would often witness her father physically beating her mother. As she revisited those moments in her mind, she described moments of her watching television or playing a game only to see her father physically abuse her mother. Now her father is elderly and is in need of around the clock care. He now exhibits the same level of vulnerability, just like her mother exhibited when she was a little girl. In reality, she could take out her childhood hurts and pain on her father in his vulnerable state, but she so desired. She shared that she harbored much resentment at her father. She cringed at the thought of helping the man that not only abused her mother, but also changed her perception of male-to-female relationships. In the quest of healing her own wounds, she asked her father, why did he ever abuse her mother and expressed how witnessing those experiences literally changed her life. She allowed forgiveness and humility to help her in her healing.

Many times, we overlook the traumatic experiences of our past and ignoring the connection between our past, current behavior and life perspective. All of us have suffered, in a suffering world, with a suffering generation and for some, a suffering community.

As humans we all need to go beyond all of our other roles leaving ourselves open to the idea that other human beings have experienced the same wounds and suffering. In other words, you are responsible for healing from your own wounds. Your wounds are your vital to your healing and your weakness can still participate in the healing of others. It's only in your brokenness can relationships be transformed before God and others.

"Forgiveness is the name of love practiced among people who love poorly. The hard truth is that all people love poorly. We need to forgive and be forgiven every day, every hour increasingly. That is the great work of love among the fellowship of the weak that is the human family." Henri J.M. Nouwen

You may be in a relationship with someone who is wounded just as you have been while the both of you express your hurt through your behavior and attitude in the relationship. The fact that God has given women the original task of being the help-make and companion of men; he has also given us an unspoken task of being wounded healers through our ability to nurture. I am not trying to convince you that your hurts are less important, however, someone has to take the initiative to heal their own wounds so they can teach others how to heal themselves. One of my friends whom I have often given relationship advice to would always ask, "Why do I have to be the one who has to take the initiative in changing the relationship?" Well, it's time to stop wearing our wounds and pride on the outside and move toward developing a selfless love. The same love that God shows toward us.

Healing your own wounds is not just a team effort for you and your partner, but an effort for you and God. It's a big difference bleeding on yourself and allowing your wounds to bleed on someone else. In chaotic moments in relationships, wounded people who have not sought out to heal their own wounds usually divert to old behaviors as a defense mechanism to protect themselves emotionally. For example because I was always a detacher, when I would argue with my husband, I would detach emotionally and "push" myself away so that I could protect my feelings and vulnerability. This caused my husband to do the same thing. It was a never-ending cycle until I decided to focus on the spiritual and emotional healings of my old wounds.

Being a wounded healer has much responsibility. First, you have to revisit your past to see if there is anything that you haven't gotten over: areas of un-forgiveness, resentment, bitterness, abuse, hopelessness etc, and take the lead to begin your healing process.

How can you begin the process of healing your own wounds?

1) Start by forgiving and letting go of grudges. If need be, speak to the people who have offended you and tell then what they have done, how they have affected you and the reason why you are forgiving them.

2) Understand that you cannot change the past, all you can do if build and learn from it.

3) Start everyday with the ideas and approach of selfless love.

A wounded person only can see their wounds, but a wounded healer can see and feel empathy for the wounds of others. In recognizing your own wounds you develop strength that is self empowering which allows you to help others while you are in your process of healing.

While writing this chapter I thought, about the parallelism between healing process of emotional wounds and physical wounds like cuts, scrapes etc. According internet medical reports physical wound healing is an intricate process in which the skin repairs itself after an injury. For example, in normal skin, an inner or deeper layer exists in steady state, forming a protective barrier against the external environment. Once the protective barrier is broken, the normal process of wound healing is immediately set in motion. Wound healing is a complex and dynamic process with the wound environment changing with the changing health status of the individual.

The phases of wound healing[13] are:
∂ Hemostasis: a complex process, which causes the bleeding process to stop. It refers to the process of keeping blood within a damaged blood vessel (the opposite of hemostasis is hemorrhage).

∂ Inflammation: The main purpose of inflammation, this immensely complex response seems to be to bring fluid, proteins, and cells from the blood into the damaged tissues.

∂ Proliferation or Granulation: the growth or production of cells by multiplication of parts or reproduction of new parts, cells, etc. this stage starts approximately four days after wounding and usually lasts until day 21 in acute wounds depending on the size of the wound.

∂ Remodeling or Maturation: Once the basic structure of the house is completed interior finishing may begin. It is the same practice in wound repair. The healing process involves remodeling the dermal tissues to produce greater tensile strength. Remodeling can take up to 2 years after.

It is apparent when dealing with physical wounds that after the wound is caused, the body automatically begins the healing process. When dealing with emotional wounds, for many people, the healing process never begins leaving the body in an unhealthy state. We have to set in place an emotional healing process for our emotional wounds by using the same wound healing process as our physical bodies.

---

[13] Kerstein , Morris D. "The Scientific Basis of Healing." Advance Wound Care 10 (1997): 30-36.

The moment that you let God initiate your healing process is the moment when true liberation can take place. Remind yourself that you cannot relive the past and that your future is far more important. Work at being proactive, not reactive.

#theworshipper

"Solitude begins with a time and a place for God, and God alone. If we really believe not only that God exists but also that God is actively present in our lives-- healing, teaching and guiding-- we need to set aside a time and space to give God our undivided attention"

Henri Nouwen

A professor in a class that I had recently taken made a powerful statement on the first day of class. He said when you are alone, and its silent your mind either drifts to a hope or a burden.

As I pondered on his thought, he ventured off to express the purpose and power of spending time with God alone. Over time, I have realized that prayer and taking time to spend with God is not about me having a one way conversation with telling Him about my wants, cares and desires. It was about true relationship!

If your best friend only called you when she/he only needed something, you would call them a user or if she/he talked the entire time and you didn't have the chance to speak one work what good is the conversation. That's how you have to look at your relationship with God. Do you ever listen when you and God talk? Do you ever allow yourself private time with God to hear what he has to say about you and your life? Do you ever just spend time with God and don't say a word but only listen?

There is a difference between criminal solitary confinement and spiritual solitary confinement. Criminal solitary confinement is a special form of imprisonment in which a prisoner is denied freedom or is given only limited contact with any other persons, though often with the exception of members of prison staff. It is an imprisonment where all freedom, choice, independence, and liberty has been taking away. Spiritual solitary confinement is a being held captive by a God, a guard who offers freedom, free will, liberation and love. The difference between the imprisonment of solitary confinement and spiritual solitary confinement is that one offers oppression while the other offers liberation.

What I learned is that there is power in prayer. Let your private prayer and worship focus point be on you and your relationship with God and no other relationship, care or concern. Through many conversations many women have prayed to God to change the behavior of their partner. Change your prayer that God may change you to be better.

"If you respect, love and value God, you worship hard, if you respect God's word, you love and value His people."
B. W. Blocker

Your relationship with God is the most important relationship you can ever have. He knows everything about you and your future. How can you ever know what God has in store for you if you don't ever listen in prayer? Many believers struggle the most in this area. We pray, expecting to hear the answer immediately from God regarding our situation especially if is an urgent. Usually when we don't "hear" or feel a response, it affects our faith or we proceed with like with our own interpretation of what we think God answer would be. What I can tell you is that when you spend much time with God you will begin to hear from Him and if you are too busy to spend time with God then you will hear little or nothing from Him.

It's almost ridiculous to think that you will be able to recognize the voice of someone whom you never take the time to hear. God has tons of things to say to us but we are usually deafened by the chaos, family and relationships. In John 10:27,

Jesus said that "My sheep hear My voice, and I know them, and they follow Me."[14] Well, do you?

True worship just doesn't happen only on Sunday morning. It's a life style and the worship experience can happen every day. Spending alone time with God and reading His word proves to Him that you are invested in the relationship.

Here are some tips:

Choose a Time: Select a time that works best with your schedule and be consistent. Give God unoccupied time. God's time only belongs to Him.

Choose A Location: The location where you have your quiet time is important. A closet, small room or corner of your home, you need a place of quiet. Bring some candles, bible and a journal. Remember that your place should be not only special, sacred and secluded. This is a place where you can be alone where you will not be disturbed or interrupted.

Read the Bible: Pick a place to start. Read it slowly and repeatedly then meditate on it. Meditate, memorize and reflect Write down what you think that God is speaking to you.

Pray: After God has spoken to you through His Word, speak to Him in prayer . This is your part of the conversation and developing an authentic relationship with God. Remember to be patient, relax, and wait on God.

---

[14] John 10:27 NKJV

#theinitiator

"The Architect of Building Your Own Happiness"
Chapter 13

A woman is like a tea bag: you cannot tell how strong she is until you put her in hot water.

Nancy Reagan

About eight years ago, I was at a point in my life where I struggled with living 1500 miles away from home, away from family, great food and feeling alone. This was the beginning of my ride on my very own personal emotional rollercoaster. During that period, I was having a conversation with my future husband that I just wasn't happy and that he needed to make me happy. Little did he know, his response literally changed my life! It was one of the wisest things that he had ever said. (Don't tell him I said that☺) He said to me, "Brandi, I will never make you happy. That's something you have to do for you!" I couldn't understand what he meant. I was devastated, and cried like a baby. A few years passed and I felt the same way until I was praying and mediating one day. I asked God to show me my own flaws and to help me to make me happy! Little did I know my husband was absolutely right! He was not responsibility to make me happy; God revealed to me that this was MY job.

In prayer, I realized that if I believe in a God that promises me an abundant life, one of happiness, stress free, drama free, unable to be used and abused by others, joy, high expectations, peace of mind, financial breathing room and everything your little heart desires. It's up to you to structure your life in order to be in position to receive them.

You determine how you will experience your own life. Not your husband, partner, children, job, friends, money, clothes, nice handbags or cars etc. It's important to recognize that happiness is not connected to wealth, fame, status, achievement. It's determined by YOUR perspective on life and the quality of your relationships with others.

Nobody is happy all of the time, but some people are definitely more fulfilled than others. You have to eliminate conditions that you place on your happiness to be an initiator:

∂ I am unhappy because ...
∂ How can I be happy when ...
∂ I will be happy when...

Putting emotional prerequisites on your happiness means you cannot be happy now and you won't be happy until your conditions are met. The flaw in this is that once your conditions are met, new ones are set. It's a never ending cycle and your entire life will be live in pursuit of happiness. We need to exercise faith more often. Learn to speak things into existence and believe that with God's help, that they will manifest. No human being should be 100% pessimistic or 100% optimistic. There is no balance in being 100% one thing. Even in the faith of a believer, 50% of faith is based on things that are unseen; the other 50% is based on how we experience life.

If one approach to life is either pessimistic or optimistic there is no balance. We have to learn how to be true to ourselves and still honor our past while developing a better you for future relationships. Your happiness and positive energy has the power to influence your partner and the people around you.

I have witnessed the most positive people say completely negative things to and about their spouse and/or relationship. Remember that negative energy breeds negativity and positive energy breeds positivity. Your mood will determine your relationship approach and how you communicate with others. For example, imagine that you had a great day at work; your boss gave you a ten thousand dollar raise and promotion; you find a coupon for a free lunch at your favorite lunch place; you go home and find that your partner has cooked, cleaned and has dinner waiting when you enter the room. You probably would be thinking, "Dag, this is my lucky day!" Your mood would be one that is extremely positive; pleasant that displays an exuberating life. If anyone met you on that day they probably would say that you are the most pleasant person that they have ever met. In all, what I am trying to say is that those exciting moments are not responsible for your happiness; you are in control of that. They just complement a natural human emotion that. Remember that the enemy can only steal your joy and happiness only if you it him.

Pink Golden Nuggets:

∂ Get rid of all traits of optimism. Figure out what is important to you in life. Focus on what is positive about yourself, others and life in general, instead of dwelling on the negative.

∂ Evaluate your life style. Think about times when you have felt happy, good or content. Where were you? Who were you with? What were you doing, thinking or feeling that made you feel happy? To be happy, you have to make happiness a priority in your life.

∂ Look at your attitude. Do your thoughts make you happy?

∂ Set the right personal goals. Decide to make more time in your life to do more of what is important to you and makes you feel happier. To be happy, you have to make happiness a priority in your life.

∂ Appreciate what is working in your life right now. In addition, develop a great support team of friends and/or family.

As you begin your journey of change keep in mind and be aware of what roles you are playing at all times. Remember you are in control of your life, your relationships and your happiness.